Stars and

by Mart

PEARSON

Scott
Foresman

DK

What is the history of astronomy?

Patterns in the Sky

Patterns are events that happen again and again over time. Two examples of patterns are the changing of seasons and the phases of the Moon. Long ago people saw many patterns in the sky. Some people made up stories about the patterns. Others invented calendars based on the cycles they came to expect.

It was useful for farmers to be able to predict the change in seasons. It helped them to know when to plant their crops. They also wanted to know when to hold festivals. So they learned to look for certain stars at certain times. Sometimes people saw surprising things, such as new objects in the sky. They thought these surprises had special meaning.

Eclipses

A solar eclipse happens when the Moon blocks the Sun's light. A lunar eclipse takes place when Earth casts a shadow on the Moon.

Eclipses are rare. They were not part of the sky patterns that early people usually saw. These people gave eclipses special meaning. Some believed that eclipses meant that something bad would happen.

Ancient leaders found that it helped to know when an eclipse would take place. But they could predict an eclipse only by carefully observing the sky. They recorded the exact movements of the Sun and the Moon. People in Asia, the Middle East, and South America recorded their observations of eclipses.

Stonehenge is about thirty meters wide. Some of its stones weigh fifty tons and are more than nine meters tall.

Astronomy Around the World

Many groups of people left no written records of their study of the sky. But some of them left behind great structures. The structures show how important astronomy was to the people.

You may have heard of a giant stone circle called Stonehenge. This structure stands in a field in England. People first began to build Stonehenge about 5,000 years ago. Work stopped and started many times. It took about 1,500 years to complete the structure.

In North America there are stone circles similar to Stonehenge. One of the best known is the Big Horn Medicine Wheel, near Sheridan, Wyoming.

Only parts of Stonehenge still stand today. It once had an outer circle of 30 huge blocks of stone. Other large slabs of stone sat horizontally on top of them to form a ring. Inside the circle was a smaller circle. It had about sixty stones. Inside that circle were still more stones. They made a horseshoe pattern.

Most scientists believe that the stone circles had something to do with astronomy. The people who built them must have understood the cycles of the Sun and the seasons. Some stones point to where the Sun rises and sets on the longest day of the year. Some stones mark the rising of the Sun or the Moon at other times of the year.

Long ago, there were clever sky watchers in the area that is now Mexico. About 700 years ago, they built an amazing four-sided pyramid. The pyramid still stands in a place called Chichén Itzá.

Each side of the pyramid has 91 steep steps to the top. If you add up the steps on all four sides, plus the platform on top, you get 365. This is the same as the number of days in a year.

One day each spring and fall, the day and the night are exactly the same length. In the late afternoon on those days, sunlight and shadows form a pattern on the pyramid that looks like a snake slithering down the steps. Scientists wonder if this pattern had a special meaning. It might have marked the time for ceremonies related to farming.

Chichén Itzá

Early Tools

People have invented many tools to learn more about the stars. One of these tools was the astrolabe. People in Europe and in the Middle East used the astrolabe for almost 2,000 years before 1700. This tool had a star map on a metal plate. Its movable parts let a user measure the angle between the horizon and an object in the sky. A user could move other plates to show how the sky would look at a certain time or in a certain place.

Newer tools came into use by the 1700s. One of these tools was the sextant. It also measures the angle between the horizon and a point in the sky. A sextant has a movable arm, mirrors, and an eyepiece. These parts attach to a frame shaped like a piece of pie.

People used the astrolabe to find the time. They could also use it to predict the times of sunrise and sunset. Sailors could use it to find their position at sea.

Early Telescopes

Galileo explains his ideas.

The telescope changed astronomy forever. Telescopes make objects in the sky look bigger and closer. The Italian scientist Galileo Galilei (1564–1642) did not invent the telescope. But he was the first person to use one for astronomy.

Galileo saw mountains on the Moon. He discovered four moons circling the planet Jupiter. Galileo also saw that Venus had phases like the Moon has.

At the time, most people believed that the Sun and the planets revolved around Earth. Galileo did not agree. Based on his discoveries, he believed that Earth and the other planets revolved around the Sun. This idea made people angry. They believed that Earth was at the center of the universe. It took many years for people to accept Galileo's new idea.

Another great scientist was born in the year that Galileo died. His name was Isaac Newton. He made the first reflecting telescope. It used a curved mirror instead of lenses. It let people see dim objects that were far away and it showed details more sharply.

Early telescopes

Today's High-Tech Telescopes

Telescopes collect light and focus it. The more light that gets to our eyes, the brighter an object will seem. The light we see from the Sun or the stars is called visible light. This is just a fraction of all the light energy in the universe.

Most objects in space give off a lot of electromagnetic radiation. This type of energy includes radio waves, infrared waves, ultraviolet waves, X rays, and gamma rays. We cannot see these rays and waves. Special telescopes do "see" different types of radiation. Observing different types of radiation helps scientists learn more about the universe.

Some modern telescopes are very large. Keck I and Keck II are two huge twin telescopes. The Kecks tie the record as the largest telescopes in the world. They gather large amounts of visible light and infrared radiation. Each has a main mirror that is 10 meters wide. The main mirrors are made of 36 smaller mirrors that work together. Astronomers use the Kecks to study very dim and distant stars.

Keck I and II were built on a mountaintop in Hawaii. They are far from city lights.

Radio Telescopes

Many objects in space give off radio waves. Radio telescopes can pick up these waves. Radio telescopes have bowl-shaped dishes that look like satellite dishes. The dishes collect and focus radio waves.

Some radio telescopes may have many smaller dishes arranged in a group called an array. The array covers the same amount of space as one giant dish might cover . It works as one system to do the work of a much larger dish.

This is a radio telescope in Puerto Rico. It is the largest single-dish radio telescope in the world. Its dish is over three hundred meters across.

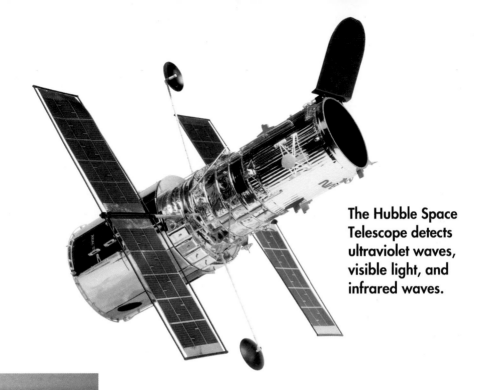

The Hubble Space Telescope detects ultraviolet waves, visible light, and infrared waves.

Telescopes on Earth must look at stars through the gases of the atmosphere. This can make the images look fuzzy. Our atmosphere blocks most types of electromagnetic radiation.

But conditions in space are always clear and dark. They are perfect for seeing stars at all times. So some telescopes are sent into space to get a better view.

You may have heard of the Hubble Space Telescope. It is the best-known space telescope. The Chandra X-Ray Observatory is another telescope located in space.

What is a star?

How the Sun Stacks Up as a Star

All stars are great balls of hot gases. Stars give off electromagnetic radiation. The Sun is a star of medium size. Stars called giants are 8 to 100 times as large as the Sun. Supergiants may be 300 times as large as the Sun. Other stars are much smaller than the Sun.

The Sun is huge compared to Earth. Picture the Sun as a gumball machine. Now think of Earth as a gumball. It would take a million little Earth gumballs to fill the Sun gumball machine!

The Sun gives off huge amounts of energy. The energy comes from reactions of the Sun's main gases: hydrogen and helium. Pressure and heat inside the Sun push the hydrogen atoms together. They combine to form helium. This process releases great amounts of energy. This is what makes the Sun shine.

There are many different sizes and colors of stars.

Brightness, Color, and Temperature of Stars

The Sun is the brightest star we see in the sky. It is also the closest. Barnard's Star is the third closest to Earth. Yet, you can't see it without a telescope. Just because a star is close does not necessarily mean it will appear bright.

The brightest stars give off the most energy. A star's distance from Earth, its size, and its temperature all play a part in how bright it looks. Sirius is a dazzling white-blue star. It is the brightest star in the night sky. But there are eight stars closer to Earth. Sirius is larger, hotter, and 20 times as bright as the Sun. It doesn't look brighter to us because it's farther away from us than the Sun is.

The color of a star tells how hot it is. Red stars are the coolest. Barnard's Star is red. A bit hotter are orange and yellow stars, such as the Sun. The hottest stars are white or blue-white, such as Sirius. But even "cool" stars are very hot. Barnard's Star is so hot that it could melt iron instantly.

There are hundreds of thousands of stars in this group of stars.

13

The Sun has no hard surfaces, but it has different layers. The part of the Sun that gives off the light we see is the photosphere. It is the lowest layer of the Sun's atmosphere. The layer above it is the chromosphere. The outermost layer is the corona.

The Sun may seem as calm as a big light bulb. But scientists see a lot of activity when they look at the Sun with special telescopes. Galileo saw dark spots moving along the face of the Sun. This showed him that the Sun rotates.

These spots, called sunspots, are part of the photosphere. They look dark because they are not as hot as the rest of that layer. The number of sunspots changes. The sunspot cycle is completed about every 11 years. Sometimes there are many sunspots. At other times, there are few.

Sunspots may be the size of Earth or larger.

Solar Eruptions

Glowing gases may leap out of the chromosphere and reach far into the corona. These blasts of glowing gas are called prominences. They can come and go in a flash, or they may last for months.

A solar flare is an event scientists link to the sunspot cycle. A solar flare takes place when parts of the chromosphere erupt like a volcano. A bright spot forms. It may last for minutes or hours. A solar flare sends out electromagnetic waves, protons, and electrons into space. This rush of waves and particles may interrupt radio signals on Earth.

Light from the Sun takes only eight minutes to reach Earth. But other stars we see are much farther away. Scientists measure how far away stars are in units called light-years. A light-year is the distance light travels in one year. Alpha Centauri is the next nearest star to Earth. It is more than four light-years away. The light we see from Alpha Centauri today was made by that star more than four years ago!

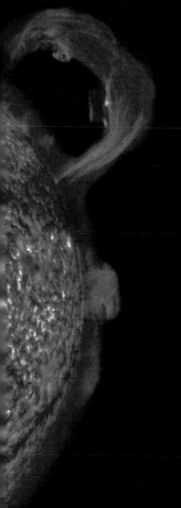

Prominences rise at great speed. They can reach enormous distances into space.

The Life of Stars

New stars form in a cloud of gas and dust called a **nebula.** Bits of gas and dust churn around. Gravity begins to pull them into the nebula and squeezes them into a ball. Gravity becomes stronger. More and more particles get pulled in. The temperature rises and hydrogen starts to change into helium. This gives off lots of energy. The nebula becomes a star.

Stars live a very long time, but not forever. In billions of years, the Sun will use up its hydrogen. It will grow thousands of times brighter. It will get 170 times its size now.

As the Sun expands, its temperature will fall. It will look red, not yellow. At that point, it will use helium for fuel. When the helium is gone, the Sun will shrink to about the size of Earth. Its layers of gas will float into space. The Sun will become a white dwarf star. It will have no fuel to make energy. Over several million years, a white dwarf slowly cools. It becomes a cold object called a black dwarf.

These fingers of gas and dust are part of the Eagle Nebula, which is 7,000 light-years away. Inside these dusty towers, new stars are forming.

When a large star suddenly runs out of fuel, it starts shrinking. It stops when it can no longer shrink. Powerful shock waves from this sudden stop fan out. Particles of matter shoot into space, releasing huge amounts of energy. A huge explosion takes place. It can be billions of times as bright as the star ever was. This explosion, known as a **supernova,** throws matter and energy far out into space. Only a ball of neutrons about 20 kilometers across is left.

If the core of the star was very large—larger than three Suns—the core's own gravity will keep making it shrink into itself. It turns into a black hole. A **black hole** is a point in space where gravity is very strong. It is so strong that nothing within a certain distance of a black hole can escape getting pulled in. Not even light can escape!

The bright star in the ring is about to become a supernova. The ring and nearby clouds are debris ejected from the star's poles and equator.

These are young stars.

Stars are forming in these clouds.

How are stars grouped together?

Galaxies

A **galaxy** is a huge system of stars, dust, and gas. Gravity holds it together. Our solar system is part of a galaxy called the Milky Way. There are billions of galaxies in the universe. Only a few can be seen without a telescope. They are so far away that they look like single points of light.

Using powerful telescopes, astronomers have found that galaxies come in different shapes and sizes. Most known galaxies are spiral galaxies. They look like pinwheels that bulge in the middle. Thin arms fan out from the center. The stars in the arms of the galaxy circle the bulge, just as Earth circles the Sun.

Elliptical galaxies can be nearly round or more oval-shaped. The largest galaxies we know are elliptical. There are some much smaller than our Milky Way.

Irregular galaxies have no real shape. Scientists believe they may be young, and their stars may still be forming.

This spiral galaxy is about 60 million light-years away. Its center contains older yellow and red stars. The arms contain large amounts of dust and young, hot blue stars.

This side view of the Milky Way shows its bulging middle and thin arms. Our solar system is near the end of an arm of the Milky Way.

This spiral galaxy is called the Sombrero Galaxy. Can you see why?

This is a young irregular galaxy. It is called the Small Magellanic Cloud. It orbits the Milky Way.

All galaxies travel through space. If two galaxies run into each other, the larger galaxy will gobble up the smaller one.

Constellations

People have always looked up at the night sky and wondered what they were seeing. They "connected the dots" of the stars into patterns. Some saw the shapes of bears, dogs, a swan, and a lion.

Scientists today divide the night sky into 88 constellations. A **constellation** is a group of stars that forms a pattern. Many constellations are named for the same star patterns people used long ago.

It is easier to study stars when you divide the sky into parts. When you know which constellation a star is in, you look in that part of the sky to find it.

Stars that seem to be close together in the same constellation may actually be very far apart. They may appear close together because they are in the same direction from Earth.

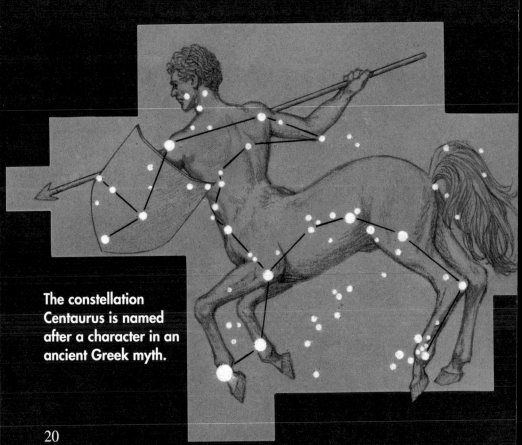

The constellation Centaurus is named after a character in an ancient Greek myth.

In the constellation Ursa Major, the Big Dipper forms the bear's back and its tail.

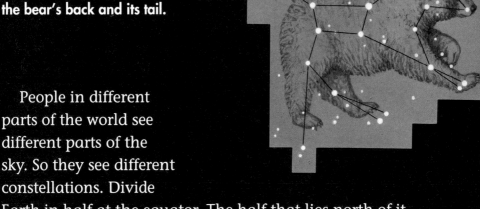

   People in different parts of the world see different parts of the sky. So they see different constellations. Divide Earth in half at the equator. The half that lies north of it is called the Northern Hemisphere. The half to the south is the Southern Hemisphere. The United States is in the Northern Hemisphere. We can see Ursa Major (Great Bear). But people in the Southern Hemisphere cannot see it.

   Look at the picture below. The ancient Greeks named this constellation Scorpius. They thought the stars made a scorpion shape. A scorpion is a small creature with a tail that gives a painful sting. If you look at Scorpius through a telescope, you will see that many of the points of light are not single stars. They are clusters of stars. The brightest single star in Scorpius is Antares. This red supergiant lies near the center of the scorpion's body.

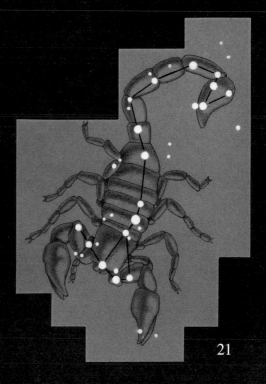

Ancient Greeks thought this star group looked like a scorpion.

Stars on the Move

Stars are always moving across the sky. But they move in ways you can predict. Suppose you look at the sky and see the Big Dipper. Two hours later, you look again. Now you see that the Big Dipper has moved to the west. In fact, the Big Dipper did not move. You moved! Earth makes one complete rotation every 24 hours. This is why the Sun seems to rise in the east and set in the west. It is also why the stars seem to move across the sky.

You can see Ursa Major, which contains the Big Dipper, all year. But you can see other constellations only at certain times of the year. Constellations change with the seasons because Earth travels around the Sun. As Earth moves, different constellations come into view. It's a bit like riding a merry-go-round. As you ride and look out, the view changes.

Nothing in the universe stands still. Stars move through space in all directions and at various speeds. Over very long periods of time, the patterns of stars will change. Stars will move closer to each other or farther apart.

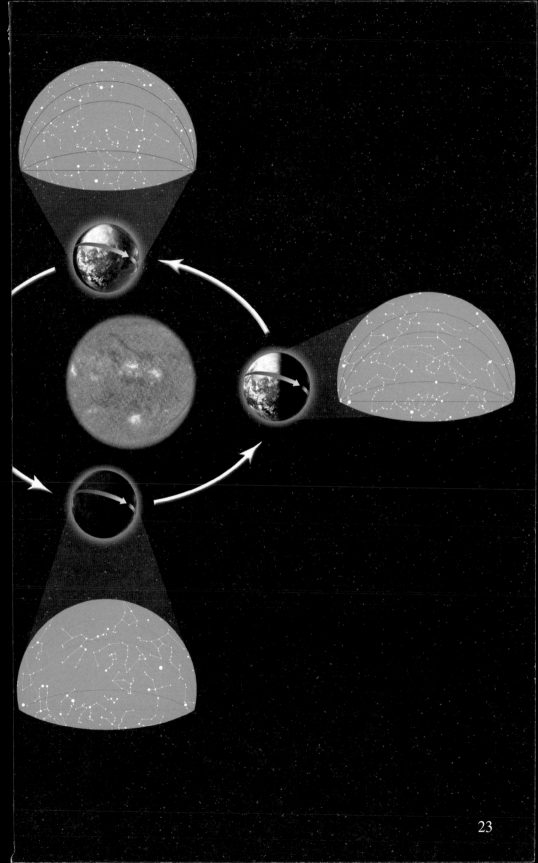

Glossary

black hole   a point in space where gravity is so strong that everything within a certain distance gets pulled in

constellation   a group of stars that forms a pattern

galaxy   a huge system of stars, planets, dust, and gas held together by gravity

light-year   the distance light travels in one year

nebula   a cloud of gas and dust in which new stars form

supernova   a gigantic explosion that occurs when a large star shrinks into itself near the end of its life